101 *must-know* ROCK LICKS

EARLY ROCK · SIXTIES · SEVENTIES · EIGHTIES · NINETIES

PLAYBACK+
Speed · Pitch · Balance · Loop

To access audio visit:
www.halleonard.com/mylibrary
Enter Code
4717-9828-6714-4538

ISBN 978-0-634-01370-6

HAL•LEONARD®
CORPORATION
7777 W. BLUEMOUND RD. P.O. BOX 13819 MILWAUKEE, WI 53213

Visit Hal Leonard Online at
www.halleonard.com

Preface

Rock is a musical language with a variety of dialects. To speak rock on the guitar with authenticity and eloquence requires more than finger dexterity, a facile mind, or a creative impulse. It requires a sense of tradition and a seemingly endless well of ideas. In non-literary cultures, the act of communication and the art of conversation is learned through what is known linguistically as "oral tradition"—a tradition passed down from generation to generation by listening, imitating, mastering, and ultimately reinterpreting with personal expression. So it is with rock. The great rock players of history have, largely by ear, studied, absorbed, and reassembled the contributions of their forebears. Picture Jimi Hendrix repeating Chuck Berry double-stop licks until they are part of his vocabulary. Or imagine Jeff Beck struggling to get Cliff Gallup's slippery riffs under his fingers. Eddie Van Halen memorized and reinterpreted Eric Clapton's and Jimmy Page's signature licks to launch the hard rock movement of the eighties. Neoclassical metalist Yngwie Malmsteen emulated and respun the progressive rock stylings of Ritchie Blackmore and married them to the music of Bach and Paganini. Slash spearheaded a nineties postmodern blues-rock renaissance with his reinventions of seventies classic rock. The process largely entails the learning and mastery of specific phrases, akin to sentences in language, or licks. This can be a daunting task considering the vast amount of musicians and styles in the genre.

Enter *101 Must-Know Rock Licks*. This book is a lexicon of essential phrases in a wide variety of styles within the rock genre. Each lick is a self-contained phrase with a central idea or focal point—an indispensable piece of the rock vocabulary. The 101 licks are presented in a roughly chronological order beginning with the fifties and continuing to the present. If you're already a rock guitar aficionado, this book may revive some delightful memories and inspire you to take your current playing down some familiar old paths. If you're coming to this guide with an interest that outweighs your knowledge of the genre, expect to be taken on a trip through the rock 'n' roll landscape, with a soundtrack to match, from which you will emerge a more conversant and passionate player.

Introduction

This special reference volume is designed for all guitarists. Arranged for quick, easy reference, it contains 101 stylistic phrases, commonly known as "licks"—those essential, self-contained instrumental figures utilized by the great masters. Licks are part and parcel of the rock tradition and the rock experience. They are short, meaningful passages skillfully tucked into songs and riffs, and laced through the solos of the repertoire. The audience may not hear them or even be aware of them, but they can always be felt. A well-turned lick can make the difference between a cold, mechanical statement and a communicative, engaging performance. The right lick driven by the energy and conviction of a seasoned player can bring the audience to its knees.

Now you can add an authentic rock feel and flavor to your playing. Here are 101 definitive licks from every major rock guitar style neatly organized into easy-to-use categories. They're all here: early rock 'n' roll, rockabilly, surf rock, blues rock, hard rock, psychedelic rock, heavy metal, progressive rock, jazz rock, alternative rock, classic rock, and more. Browse to your heart's content and feel free to tap into the feeling of each lick that speaks to you. As you do, you take the vital first step of reinvention that connects you to the spirit and the essence of the most powerful popular music of all time.

Contents

Tips for Using this Book and Audio

1. Play these licks all over the fingerboard. If a lick is positioned at the eighth fret, move it down to the third fret and play it in that area. You will notice that the string feel, tension, and fret distances have a bearing on how the lick feels. Then move it up chromatically as a drill, playing it in every position from the third to the seventeenth fret. (This will depend on the range of your guitar's fingerboard.) Note the key changes as you move the licks to different positions.

2. Put several licks into the same key. For example, if a lick is presented in C and another is in G, place them both into C and G. This is the musical equivalent of using all your linguistic phrases in one conversation.

3. Take that collection of phrases into various keys. When you have grouped a number of licks into the same key, move that grouping to new positions.

4. Make notes, mental or written, about the feel of each lick. Your visceral, emotional reaction to a lick is part of the ad-lib selection process when improvising. This process could involve forming a visual image of the lick's physical shape—how it sits on the fingerboard.

5. Add at least one new lick a week to your vocabulary. Memorize and *use it* in your current musical situation—playing with a band, adding it to an existing solo or song, jamming with your friends, and the like.

About the Recording

Each lick is played twice on the accompanying audio: first at the normal tempo, and then, after a two-second pause, at a slower tempo.

Licks 1-98 are found at the corresponding audio track numbers. Licks 99, 100, and 101 are presented as a single track 99. Within that track, use the following time codes to find the three licks: Lick 99 occurs at 0:00, Lick 100 occurs at 0:46, and Lick 101 at 1:16.

This recording marks a real point of departure from my usual studio M.O. In the past, I relied on an extensive battery of amplifiers and effects processors—usually vintage models. On this audio companion, I played all the licks on the new Fender Cyber-Twin, which contains a wide variety of authentic effects processors, an immense collection of vintage amp tones, and some presets that just knocked me out. As an aid for other Cyber-Twin users out there in the future (I am sure there will be many), I have included my basic settings and amp choices as starting points for your own tonal explorations. Many of these are stock Cyber-Twin presets with some slight tweaks, such as changes in preamp gain and added or modified effects (reverb, echo, chorus, flanging, etc.).

Licks Analysis and the Lick Legend

Licks are the musical sentences of the rock language. Part of learning, understanding, and mastering a language involves studying the "basic parts of speech." The following terms and their abbreviations are used to define these specific elements at work in the licks—they are used to diagram the rock sentences, so to speak. The abbreviations are used throughout in lieu of text blurbs to provide a streamlined but thorough approach to lick analysis.

The Lick Legend

Certain single-melody tones are cited and circled in the music notation. These include:

LT=Leading Tone. A leading tone pushes toward an important melodic tone from a half step below—in blues and rock, typically to the 3rd, 5th, or tonic note.

LN=Lower Neighbor note. A note either a half step or whole step below a principal tone.

NH=Non-Harmonic tone. These would include the 2nd or 9th, 4th or 11th, 6th or 13th, and major 7th degrees of the scale.

BN=Blue Note. These include the flatted 5th/augmented 4th, the minor 3rd in a major or dominant context, and the minor 7th.

Certain larger structural devices, such as specific figures of three notes or greater are cited and bracketed in the notation. These include:

ARP=Arpeggio (preceded by a chord name, such as "C arp.")

CA=Chromatic Ascent. Three or more chromatic notes in a row moving higher in pitch.

CD=Chromatic Descent. Three or more chromatic notes in a row moving lower in pitch.

RF=Repeated Figure. These are the basis for the riff and ostinato procedure in rock playing.

IMIT=Imitative procedure at work.

Q: and A: =Question and Answer phrases. The "call and response" procedure is an important aspect of larger rock melody structure.

Every lick is defined by an overall context; this can be a "basic scale" or "basic tonality," depending on its melodic (single notes) or chordal nature. Furthermore, the harmonic situation of each lick is described via the Roman numeral chord symbols: I, IV, V, etc. below the TAB staff. These will aid you in using the phrases purposefully against specific chord progressions. A suggested tempo is provided for each lick—Fast Rock, Moderate Shuffle, Slow Rock, etc.—to further guide you in applying these phrases to your music.

Finally, once you have grasped the essentials of lick analysis, begin your own investigations. Get out your favorite rock recordings and listen for these devices at work in the music of the greats. Be on the lookout for imitative procedures in melodies and riffs, question-and-answer phrases, unique physical techniques, and other strategies. This sort of active listening and thinking opens the door to a deeper understanding and assimilation of the rock language.

Early Rock Guitar: The Roots

The fifties marked the dawn of the rock age. This era saw the inception of the rock 'n' roll band, which evolved from the smaller swing, R&B, and blues combos of the forties. In these settings, the first phase of the rock guitar vocabulary was invented and established by innovative players like Chuck Berry, Scotty Moore, Bo Diddley, Buddy Holly, and James Burton.

Chuck Berry is widely acknowledged as the father of rock 'n' roll guitar. Berry combined various elements of blues, swing, pop, and country to form his unmistakable approach. He created and perfected a highly rhythmic, riff-dominated guitar style based on double stops and triads, bluesy string bending, and swing/jazz phrases. Berry's licks, riffs, and rhythm figures have been appropriated by countless players in the succeeding generations of rock music. In fact, it is difficult to cite a rock guitarist who hasn't been affected by Chuck in some way, so pervasive and profound is his influence. More than forty years later, Berry's legacy has endured, despite the temporary and fickle nature of pop music, and remains a cornerstone of the rock guitar heritage.

For these licks, I used a Gibson ES175D with humbucking pickups and heavy-gauge strings (wound G) and a Gibson ES335 dot-neck with light-gauge strings. The amplifier sounds are from the Fender Cyber-Twin's extensive amp collection. Several classic tweed 1950s amp tones were employed, including a Deluxe NP (Narrow Panel) '55, a Pro WP (Wide Panel) '53, a Bassman NP '59, and a Twin NP '59. These choices are indicated in the score in each section to assist you in tone shaping and effects use.

1 Basic Scale: B♭ Major/Mixolydian

Deluxe NP '55

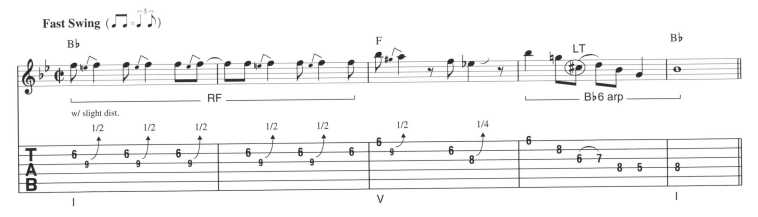

2 Basic Scale: D Mixolydian/ Blues

Pro WP '53

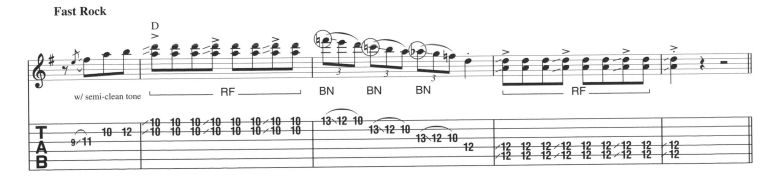

3 Basic Scale: D Mixolydian/Minor Pentatonic

Pro WP '53

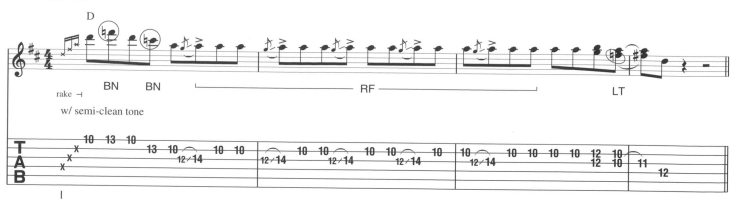

4 Basic Scale: D Blues

Pro WP '53

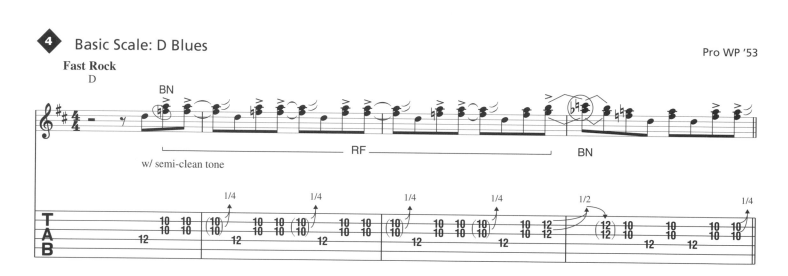

5 Basic Tonality: G Major/Blues

Bassman NP '59

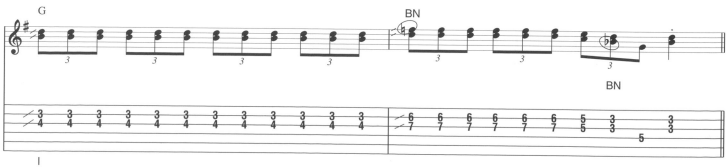

6 Basic Scale: B♭ Mixolydian

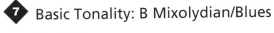

7 Basic Tonality: B Mixolydian/Blues

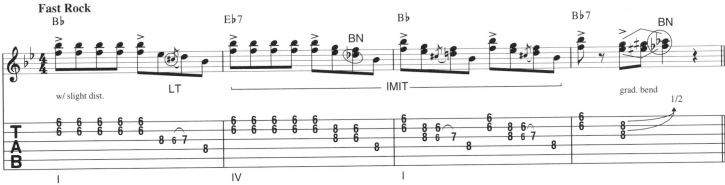

8 Basic Tonality: C Mixolydian/Blues

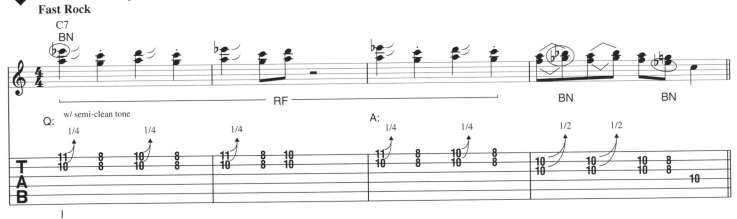

9 Basic Tonality: G Mixolydian/Blues

Early rock 'n' roll guitar was a melting pot of styles and influences. Where Chuck Berry's style epitomized the blues and R&B aspects of 1950s rock 'n' roll, the genre dubbed "Rockabilly" veered off into the country side of the equation. A contraction of rock 'n' roll and "hillbilly," rockabilly is a guitar-driven medium featuring country fingerpicking, jazzy western swing licks, boogie-woogie bass figures, and bluesy string bends. During this period, Western Swing was a prevalent musical form which drew substantially from the guitar traditions of players like Merle Travis, Chet Atkins (the "Western" part), and Charlie Christian (the "Swing" component). These ingredients were assimilated and mixed with rural blues influences from artists such as Lightnin' Hopkins and Big Bill Broonzy. The eclectic pop-jazz of Les Paul also figured prominently in the incipient rock 'n' roll equation. The resulting fusion of styles was reinterpreted by the first school of rock guitar players, and each took the music in a different direction. Noteworthy are the various contributions of Scotty Moore (with Elvis Presley), Carl Perkins, Cliff Gallup (with Gene Vincent's Blue Caps), James Burton (with Ricky Nelson), Danny Cedrone (with Bill Haley and the Comets), Paul Burlison (with the Rock and Roll Trio), Eddie Cochran, and Brian Setzer in the modern era. Also significant are the contributions of Bo Diddley, the creator the all-important "Diddley" rhythm groove, Buddy Holly, Richie Valens, and Nashville virtuoso Hank Garland.

These licks were played with a variety of "period guitars" including a '52 Fender Telecaster, a '60 Fender Stratocaster, a Gibson ES335, a Gibson ES175D, and a Gibson Les Paul Standard. The amp tones are again from the Fender Cyber-Twin. I used vintage 1950s and early 1960s tweed, brown-face, and blackface sounds, occasionally enhanced with a touch of tape echo, amp tremolo, and/or spring reverb via the Cyber-Twin's onboard effects processing.

11 Basic Tonality: A Major

Tweed Amp & Slap Echo

12 Basic Tonality: E Dominant

Tweed Amp & Slap Echo

13 Basic Tonality: D Dominant

Champ '49

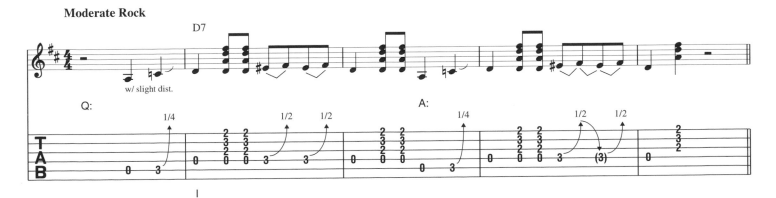

14 Basic Tonality: A Dominant

Bassman NP '59

Fast Rock

*P.M.
let ring throughout
w/ pick and fingers

* Palm mute notes on 6th & 4th strings.

15 Basic Tonality: E Major

Bassman NP '59 & Tape Echo: 125ms

Fast Shuffle

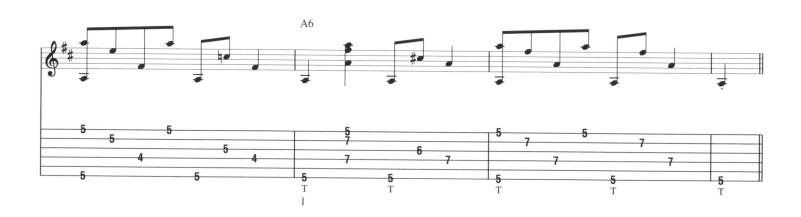

P.M.
* w/ echo
w/ pick and fingers

* Palm mute notes on 6th, 5th & 4th strings.

16 Basic Tonality: C Major

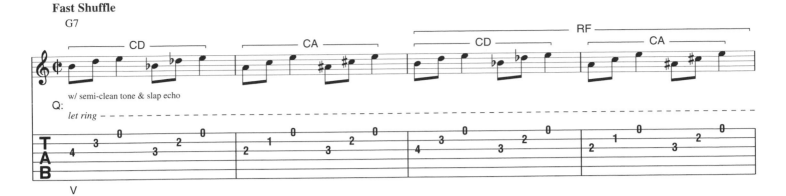

17 Basic Scale: E Mixolydian

Bassman NP '59 & Tape Echo: 150ms

18 Basic Scale: C Blues/Mixolydian

Bassman NP '59 & Tape Echo: 130ms & Reverb

19 Basic Scale: C Major

Bassman NP '59 & Tape Echo & Reverb

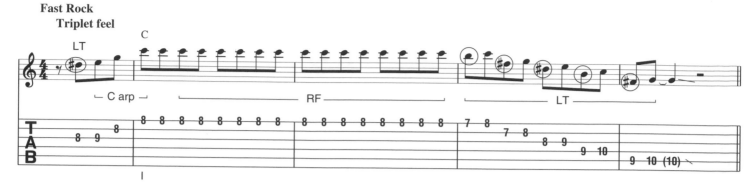

20 Basic Scale: G Mixolydian

Tremolux NP '59

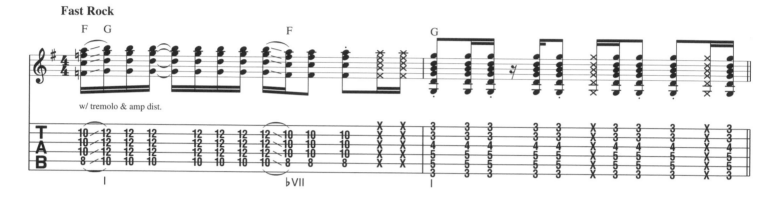

21 Basic Scale: A Mixolydian

Twin NP '59

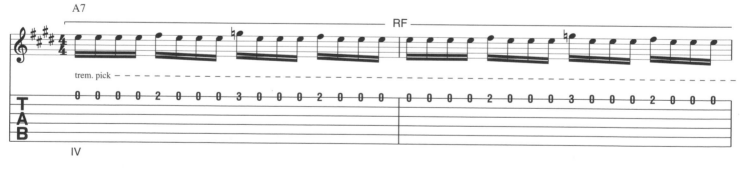

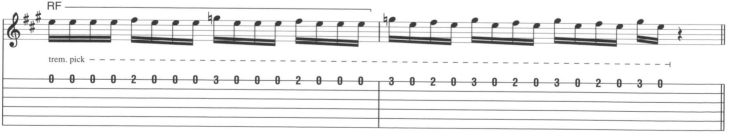

14

22 Basic Scale: E Mixolydian/Chromatic

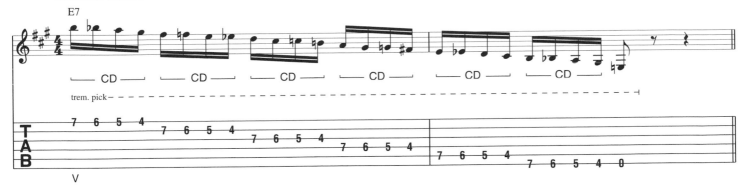

23 Basic Tonality: E Major

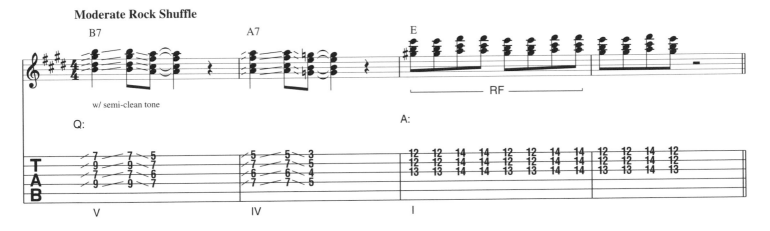

24 Basic Scale: E Mixolydian/Dorian

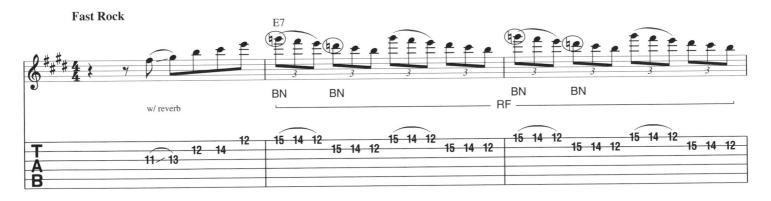

25 Basic Tonality: A Dominant

Bassman NP '59

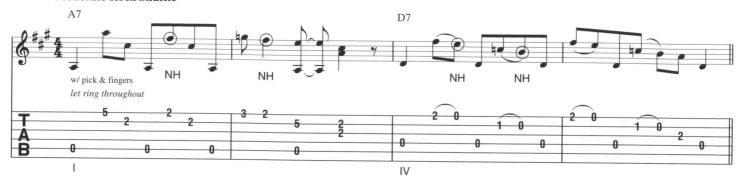

26 Basic Tonality: A Major

Pro WP '53

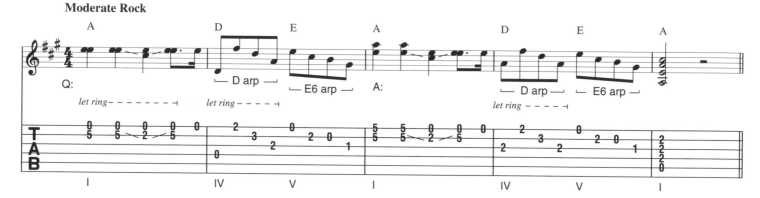

27 Basic Tonality: E Major

Bassman NP '59

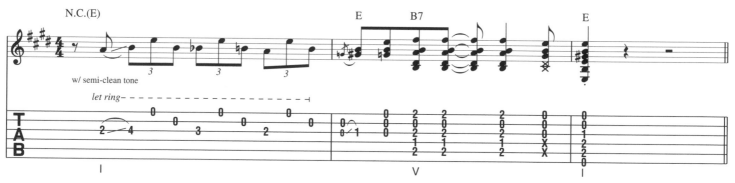

28 Basic Scale: E Dorian

Pro WP '53

16

29 Basic Scale: E Blues

Pro WP '53 & Reverb

Moderate Rock

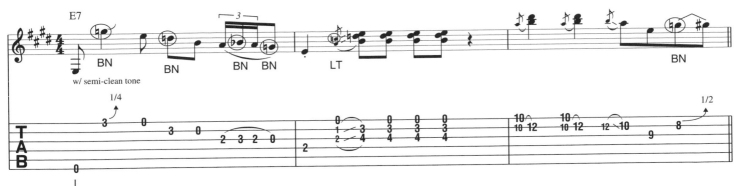

30 Basic Scale: F♯ Minor Pentatonic

Twin NP '60 Mod & Reverb

Moderate Rock Shuffle

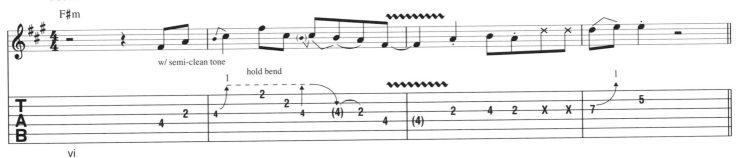

31 Basic Scale: E Minor Pentatonic

Bassman NP '59

Moderate Rock

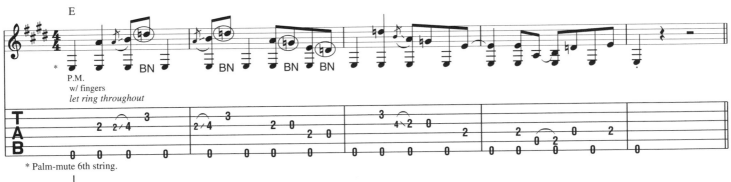

32 Basic Scale: E Blues

Pro WP '53

Moderate Rock Shuffle

The Sixties

As the fifties drew to a close, many lamented the "death of rock 'n' roll" with the passing of Buddy Holly, Richie Valens, and Eddie Cochran, the incarceration of Chuck Berry, and the induction of Elvis into the army. The rise of manufactured pop idols further strengthened the perception. Savvy rock fans knew that, although rock 'n' roll would never die, it would disappear from the pop radar scope at times. Rock guitar was kept alive in the lean years of the early sixties with resilient surf and instrumental rock groups. The leading guitarists of this period include Dick Dale, Steve Cropper (with Booker T. and the MGs), Lonnie Mack, Link Wray, Duane Eddy, and groups like The Ventures and Chantays.

For these licks, I used a Fender Stratocaster, Telecaster, and a Gibson Les Paul Standard. Amp settings are comprised of various classic late fifties and early sixties tweed, brown, and white tolex models.

33 Basic Scale: E Minor Pentatonic

Twin NP '59

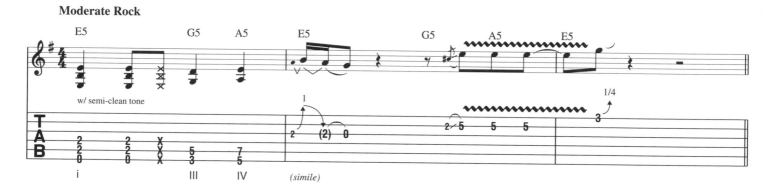

34 Basic Tonality: A Dominant

Bandmaster '60 & Reverb

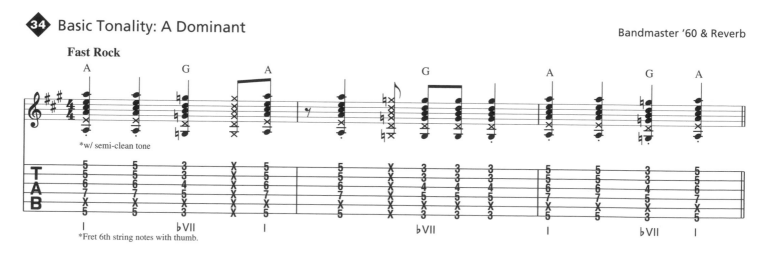

35 Basic Scale: E Major Synthetic (E–F–G#–A–B–C—D#)   Twin NP '60 Mod & Reverb Unit

Fast Rock

36 Basic Tonality: E Major   Twin NP '60 Mod & Reverb

Moderate Rock

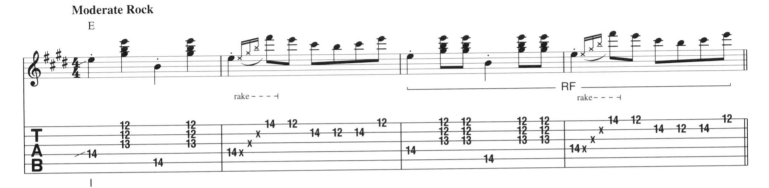

37 Basic Tonality: E Minor   Tweed Amp & Tape Echo

Moderate Rock

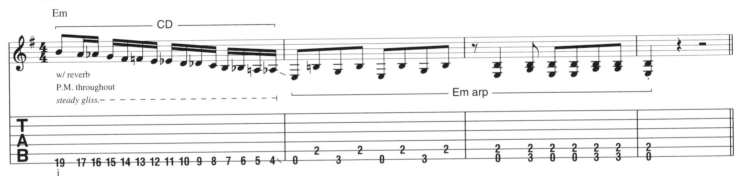

38 Basic Scale: F Minor Pentatonic   Bassman NP '58 & Reverb Unit

Fast Rock

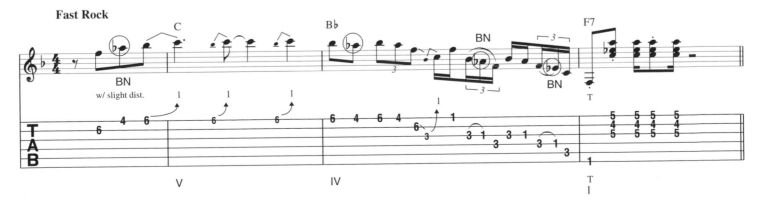

The first wave of the British Invasion (The Beatles, Rolling Stones, Animals, Kinks, The Who, etc.) embraced and repackaged many of the classic licks of rock 'n' roll, blues, rockabilly, and R&B (see previous sections), reintroducing the music of Chuck Berry, John Lee Hooker, various rockabilly cats, Buddy Holly, and Bo Diddley to a brand new pop audience.

In the mid sixites, a new strain of rock appeared in the form of the psychedelic, blues-oriented sounds of the Yardbirds, Cream, Fleetwood Mac, Ten Years After, and finally Led Zeppelin. Players like Eric Clapton, Jeff Beck, Jimmy Page, Mick Taylor, Peter Green, and Alvin Lee found inspiration in American blues music and emulated guitarists like B.B. King, Albert King, Freddy King, Buddy Guy, Otis Rush, and Elmore James, as well as the Far Eastern sounds of sitarist Ravi Shankar. This pioneering group of musicians wrote the first chapter in the textbook of modern rock guitar playing.

These licks were played on a Gibson ES335 and Les Paul Standard, and a Fender Telecaster. The amp sounds included classic tones such as Vintage Stack, Dirty Thirty, Sixties Fuzz, and Vibro-Page.

39 Basic Scale: D Blues/Major

Dirty 30 & Reverb

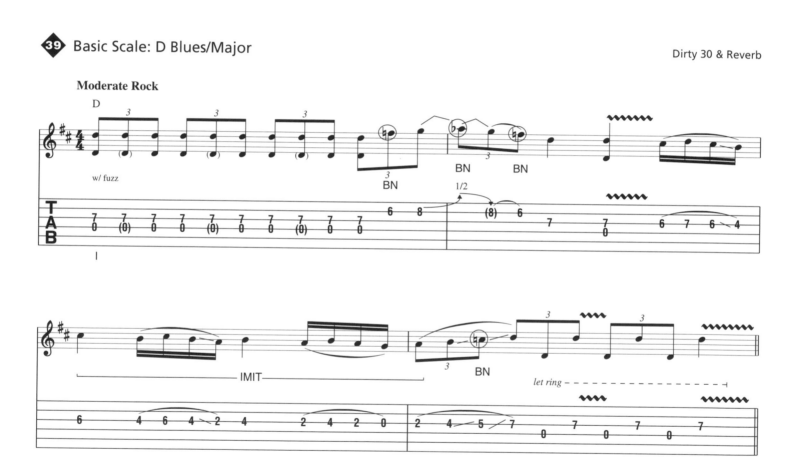

40 Basic Scale: C Minor Pentatonic

Sixties Fuzz

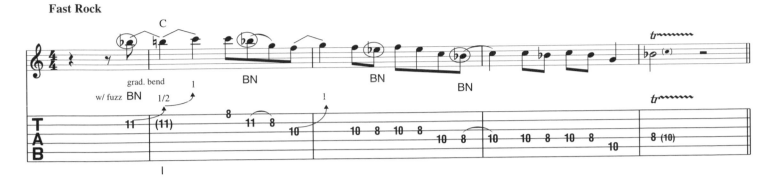

41 Basic Scale: C Mixolydian

Vintage Stack

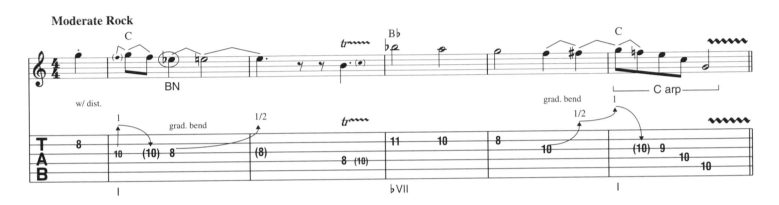

42 Basic Scale: G Mixolydian

Sixties Fuzz

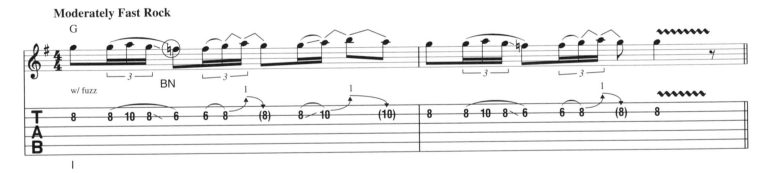

43 Basic Scale: D Minor Pentatonic/Major Pentatonic

Vintage Stack

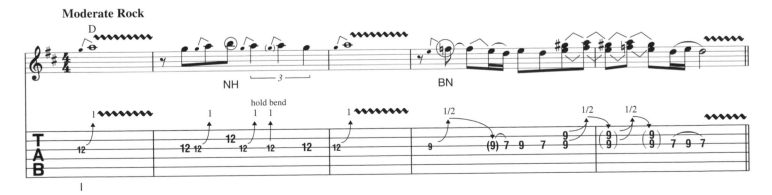

44 Basic Scale: D Minor Pentatonic/Major Pentatonic

Vintage Stack & Wah Pedal

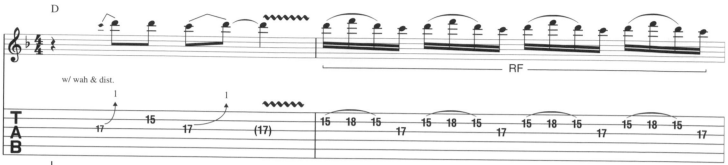

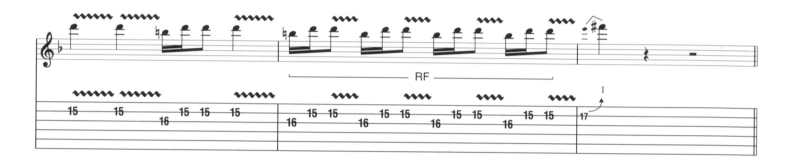

45 Basic Scale: D Major

Vintage Stack

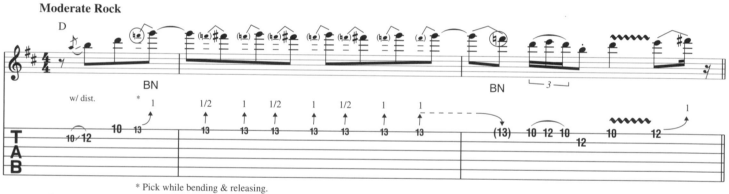

* Pick while bending & releasing.

46 Basic Scale: E Minor Pentatonic

Vibro-Page

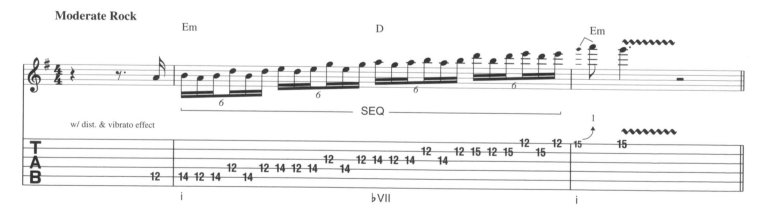

Basic Scale: A Minor Pentatonic

Free Time

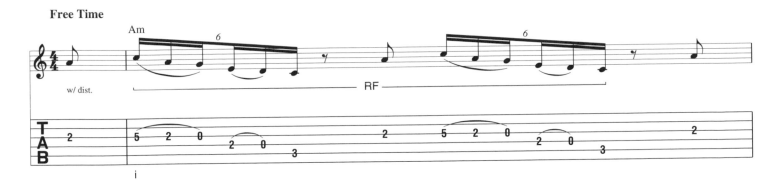

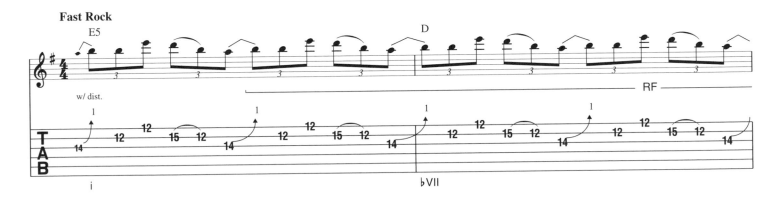

* Bend while stretching string behind the nut.

48 Basic Scale: E Minor Pentatonic

Fast Rock

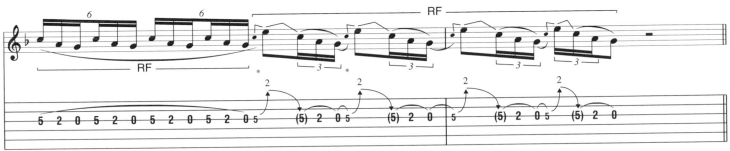

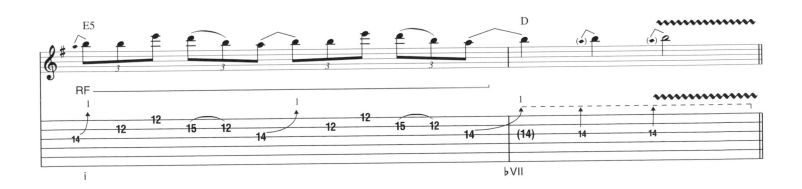

 **Basic Scale: A Minor Pentatonic**

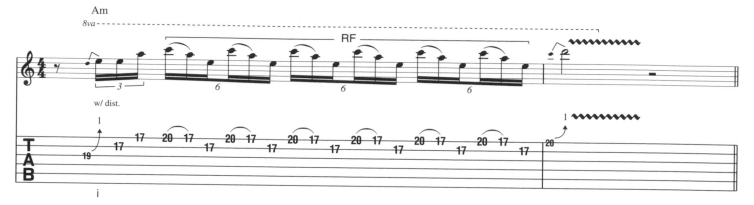

In any book on rock guitar, Jimi Hendrix must be accorded his own section. A product of the late sixties, Jimi Hendix left all subsequent musicians a towering legacy. While nowadays every guitar-ist is familiar with his contibutions, for rock guitarists his licks are required fundamentals. Hendrix was the master of blues-rock soloing and a highly influential chord-melody stylist. His approach is a unique mosaic incorporating electric blues a la T-Bone Walker and Buddy Guy, British art-rock psychedelia, Dylanesque folk rock, free-form jazz and aleatory music, and the R&B tangents of Steve Cropper and Curtis Mayfield. Robin Trower and Frank Marino are direct descendants, but all rock guitarists owe an immeasurable debt to Hendrix.

To get close to the Hendrix sound, nothing but a Fender Stratocaster will do. These licks were played on a stock Fender Strat using various single-coil settings. The amp tones include various British vintage stack settings, with and without a wah-wah pedal (also from the Cyber-Twin inter-nal effects array), and combo-amp clean sounds enhanced with vibrato effects and reverb.

50 **Basic Scale: E Minor Pentatonic**

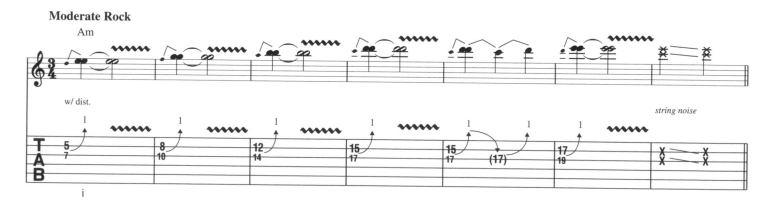

51 Basic Scale: E Minor Pentatonic

Vintage Stack

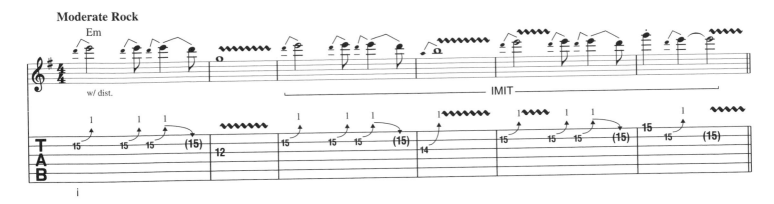

52 Basic Scale: E Minor Pentatonic

Voodoo Haze

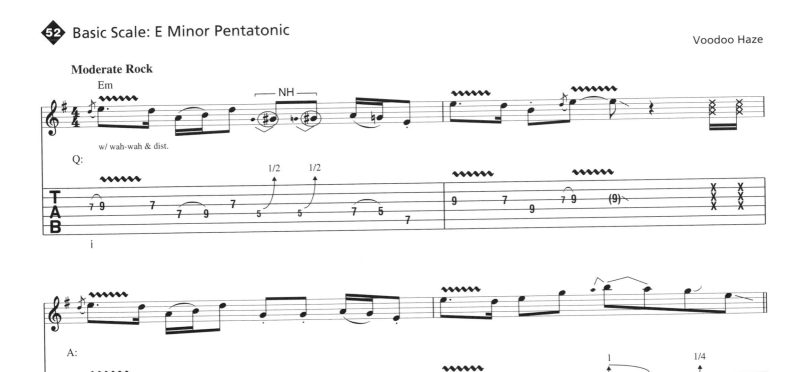

53 Basic Scale: A Minor Pentatonic

Reverb Bassman

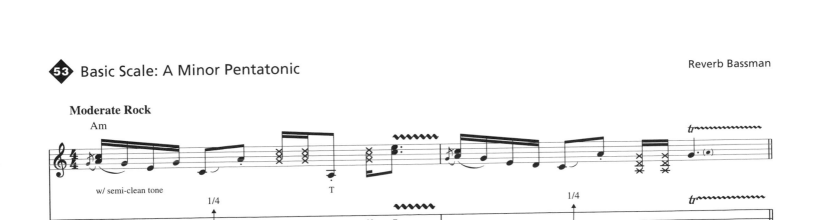

25

54 ◆ Basic Scale: C# Minor Pentatonic

Vintage Stack

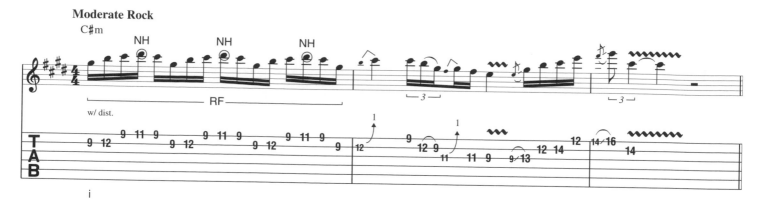

55 ◆ Basic Scale: E Mixolydian

Twin NP '59 & Reverb

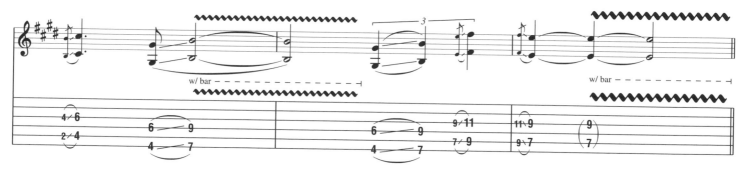

56 ◆ Basic Tonality: E Dominant

Vintage Stack

57 Basic Tonality: A Minor

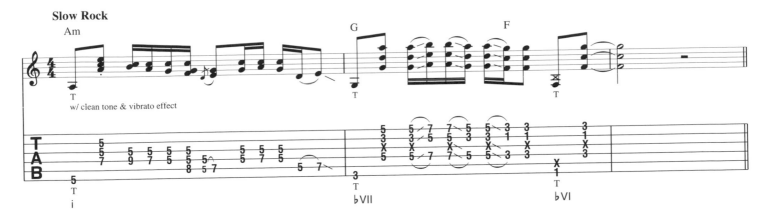

58 Basic Tonality: D Dominant

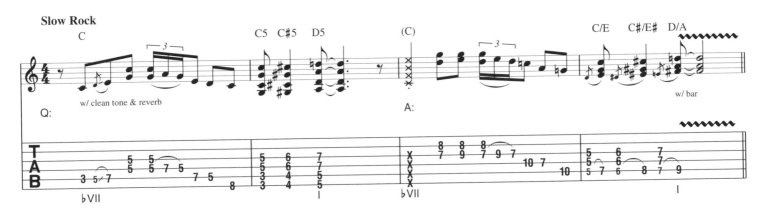

59 Basic Scale: E Minor Pentatonic

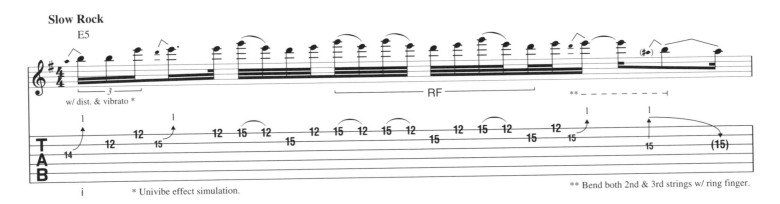

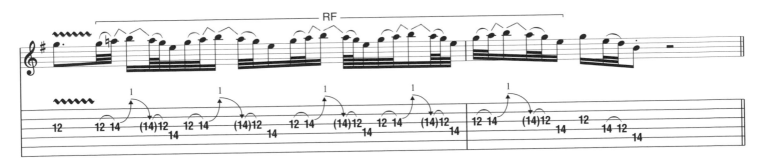

The Seventies

The rock music of the seventies picked up where the sixties left off. Several new styles surfaced and began to flourish. These included heavy metal (at first an inevitable outgrowth of the Cream-Hendrix blues-rock movement), progressive rock (a blend of hard rock, classical music, blues, and jazz), and jazz rock (initially the fusion of American jazz and British blues rock). Leading rock guitarists of the period include Carlos Santana, Ritchie Blackmore (Deep Purple and Rainbow), Tony Iommi (Black Sabbath), David Gilmour (Pink Floyd), Billy Gibbons (ZZ Top), Brian May (Queen), Joe Walsh (The Eagles), Michael Schenker (UFO), Uli Roth (The Scorpions), Allan Holdsworth, Al DiMeola, Larry Carlton, and Gary Moore.

These licks were played with a variety of instruments including a Gibson Les Paul Standard, ES335, and several Fender Stratocasters. Amp tones and effects include vintage stack, tweed, and high-gain stack sounds, colored with wah, echo, and flanging.

60 Basic Scale: D Minor Hexatonicc

High Voltage

61 Basic Scale: G Minor (Dorian)

High Voltage

62 Basic Scale: C Minor (Dorian)

63 Basic Scale: D Natural Minor

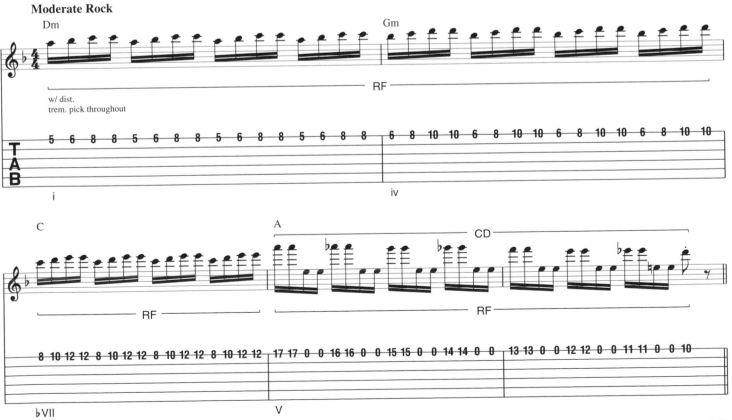

64 Basic Tonality: G Minor

High Voltage

Moderate Rock

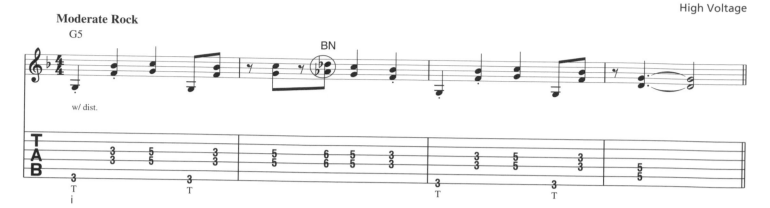

65 Basic Scale: E Minor Pentatonic

High Voltage

Moderate Rock

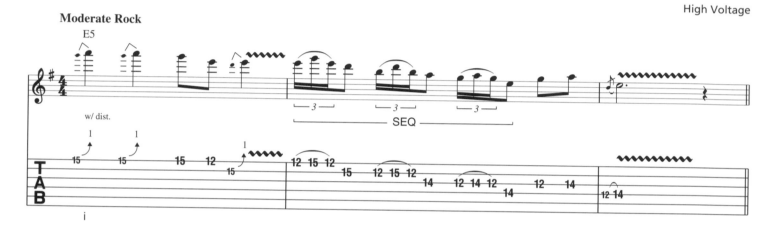

66 Basic Scale: C♯ Minor Pentatonic

High Voltage

Moderate Rock

67 Basic Tonality: A Major

Think Floyd
British Stack & Delay: 910ms.

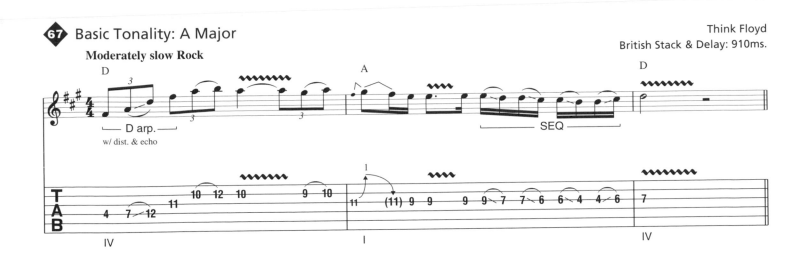

68 Basic Scale: D Minor Hexatonic

Pink Brick
Tweed Amp & Tape Echo: 455ms.

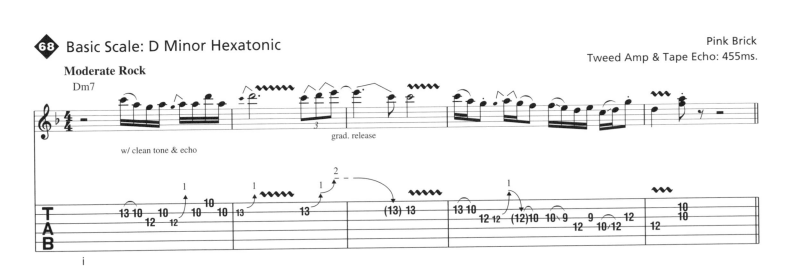

69 Basic Scale: E Natural Minor

Vintage Stack & Pedal Wah

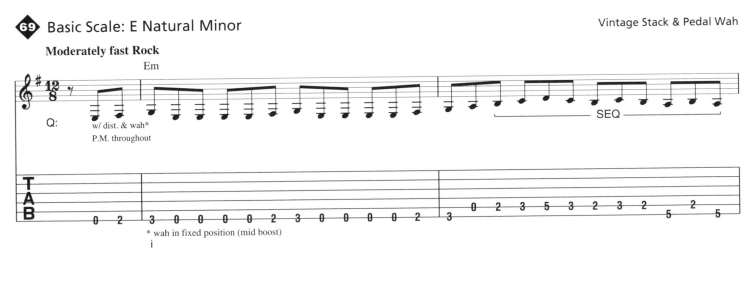

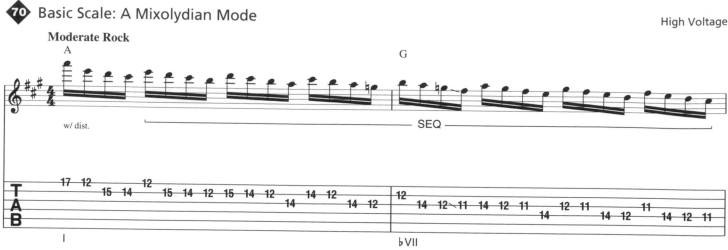

70 Basic Scale: A Mixolydian Mode

High Voltage

71 Basic Scale: G Mixolydian Mode

High Voltage & Reverb

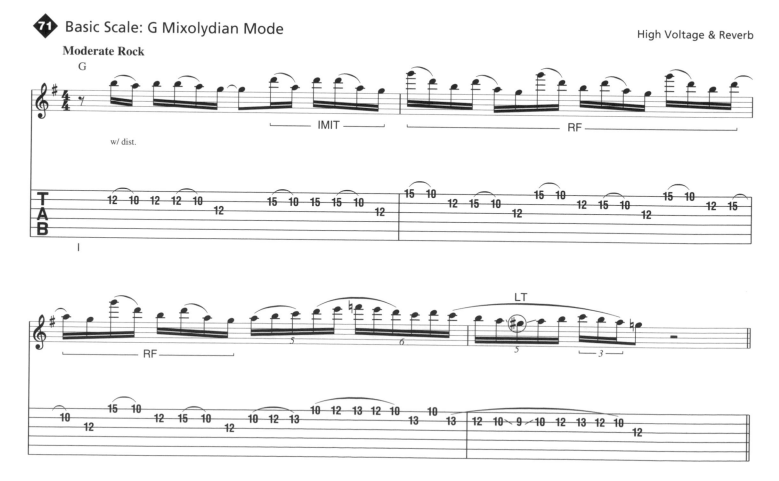

72 Basic Scale: C Major

Modern & Delay: 505ms.

Moderate Rock

73 Basic Scale: E Harmonic Minor/Natural Minor

Dual Richter

Moderate rock

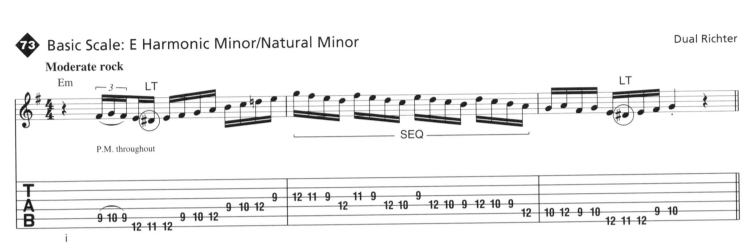

Rhapsody
British Amp & Tri Flange

74 Basic Scale: E♭ Major

Moderate Rock

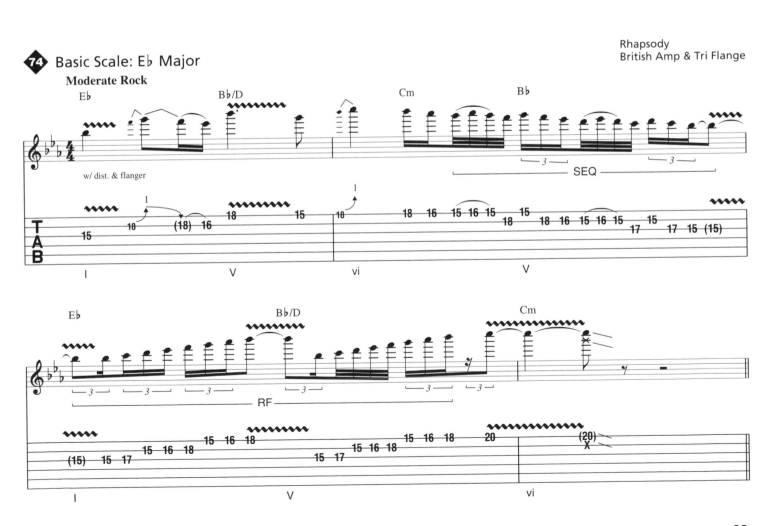

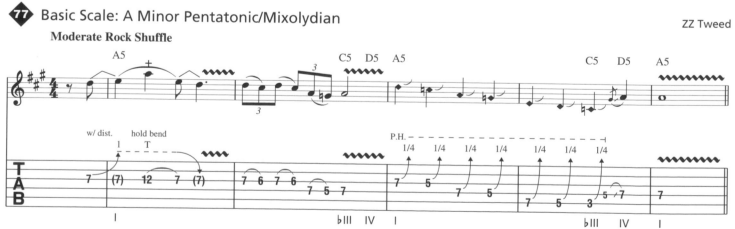

The age of the metal guitar hero began with the explosive appearance of Eddie Van Halen in 1978. His style was a brave new amalgam of progressive rock, heavy metal, and blues rock. Inspired by Eric Clapton, Jimmy Page, and Allan Holdsworth, Edward fashioned an innovative and influential approach utilizing bi-dextral tap-ons, over-the-top rock virtuosity, and an expanded use of harmonics. Van Halen's guitar style was the bridge from the sixties and seventies to the eighties. Along with Chuck Berry and Jimi Hendrix, he is considered to be one of the most important players in rock music.

I played these licks on a Fender Jeff Beck Strat with the humbucking bridge pickup engaged, or a Gibson Les Paul Standard. The amp and effects settings include the Brown Sound and Modern Stack patches with flanging, phasing, chorus, and tape echo.

78 Basic Scale: A Blues Scale

Brown Sound w/ Delay (320ms) & Flanger

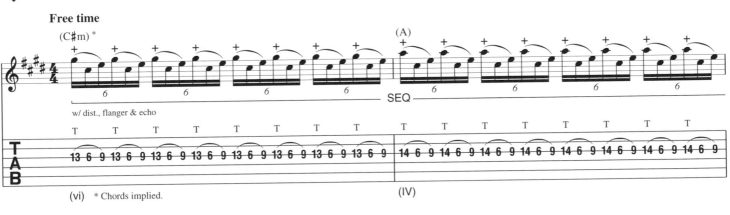

79 Basic Tonality: E Major

Brown Sound w/ Delay (320ms) & Flanger

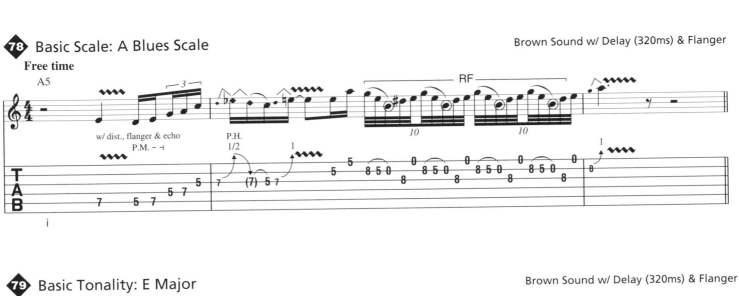

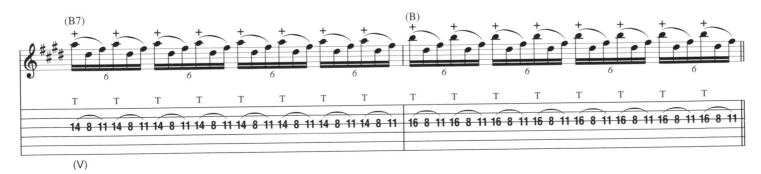

80 Basic Scale: B Mixolydian

Brown Sound w/ Tape echo (555ms)

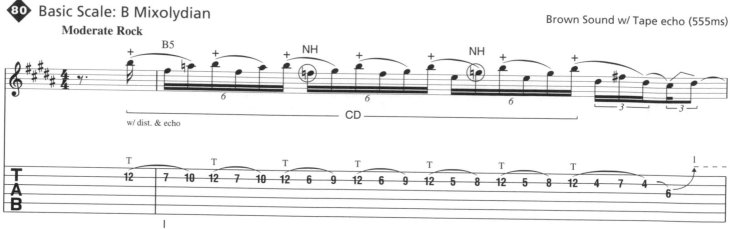

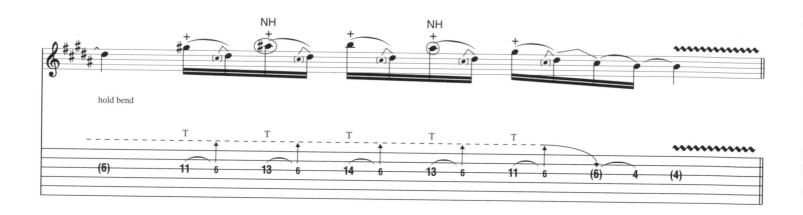

81 Basic Tonality: E Minor

Brown Sound w/ Delay (540ms) & Flanger

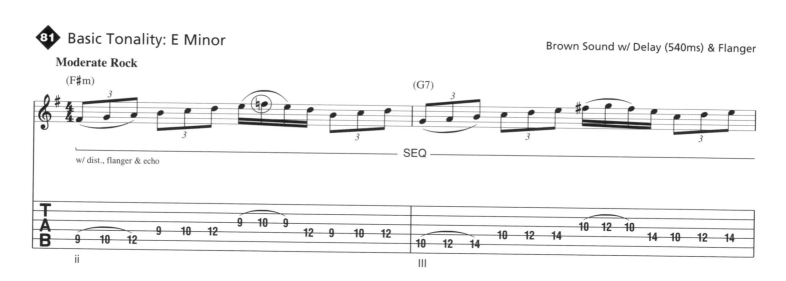

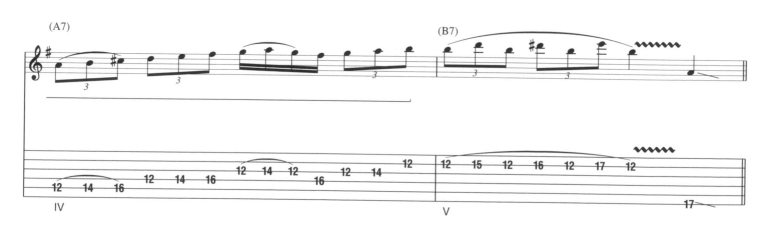

82 Basic Scale: E Mixolydian/Blues

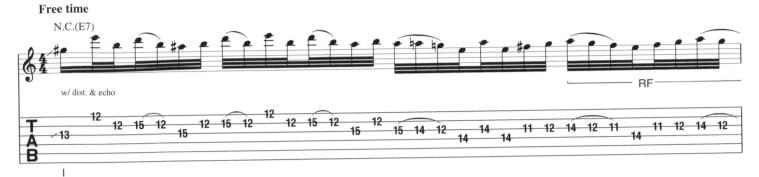

83 Basic Scale: A Blues

84 Basic Tonality: A Minor (Dorian)

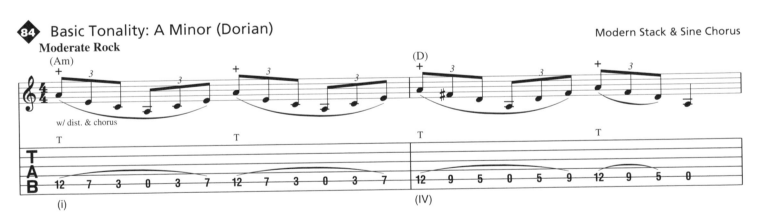

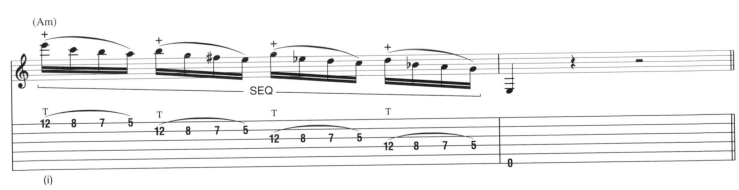

The Eighties

The eighties were a productive era for rock guitarists of every stripe. Van Halen's sweeping influence led to the L.A. "pop metal" movement with bands like Motley Crue, Ratt, Quiet Riot, and Dokken following Eddie's lead. Guitar virtuoso Randy Rhoads threw down another gauntlet and ushered in the age of Neoclassical Metal, influencing countless new groups as well as established acts like Judas Priest, the Scorpions, and Iron Maiden. Yngwie Malmsteen picked up that gauntlet and founded the full-blown Neoclassic Metal school of the mid eighties, which in turn inspired the "shred" movement. Other significant rock guitar players of the eighties include Steve Vai, Steve Morse, Joe Satriani, Steve Lukather, Kirk Hammett, and Slash.

These licks were played with a Gibson Les Paul Standard and a Fender Jeff Beck Strat. The heavy rock tones are based on either the modified modern stack ("High Voltage") settings or unique individual presets like Vaitality, Big Wet Lead, and Mista Scary.

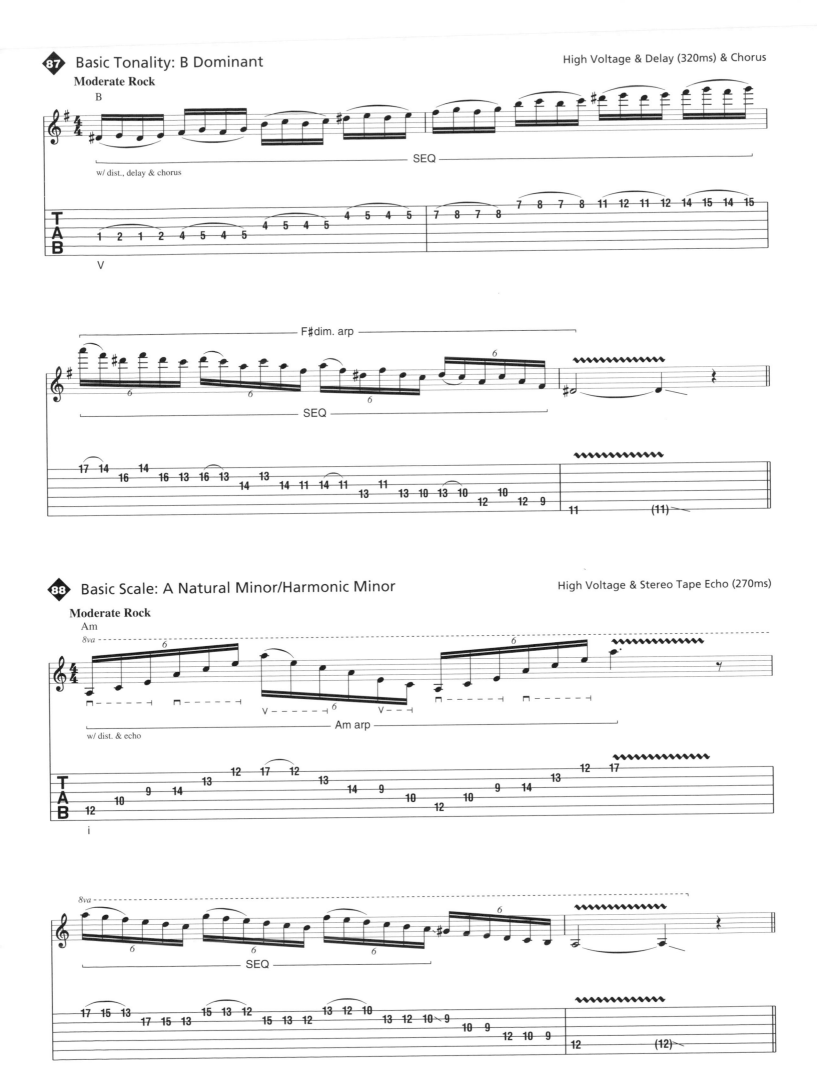

89 Basic Scale: B Natural Minor

High Voltage & Stereo Tape Echo (400ms)

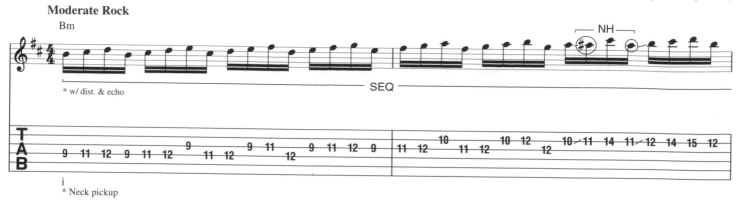

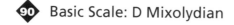

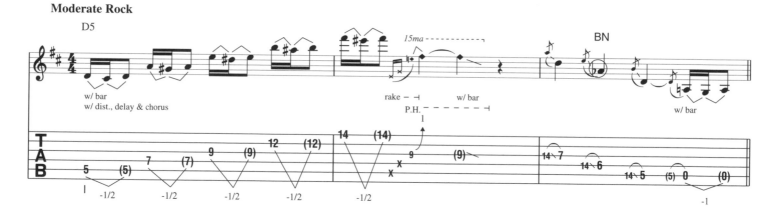

90 Basic Scale: D Mixolydian

Vaitality

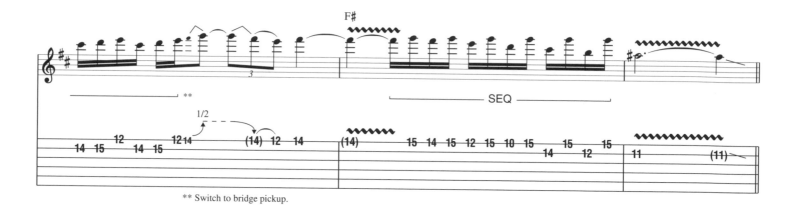

91 Basic Scale: C Mixolydian

Big Wet Lead

92 Basic Scale: D Mixolydian

Moderate Rock

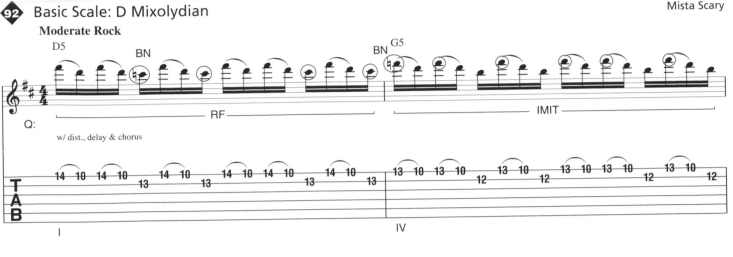

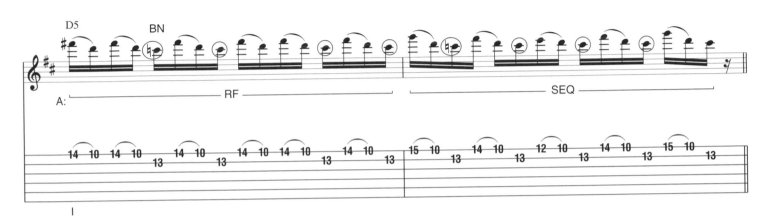

93 Basic Scale: F Mixolydian

Moderate Rock

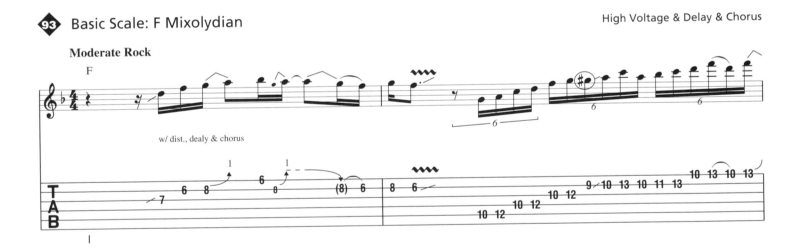

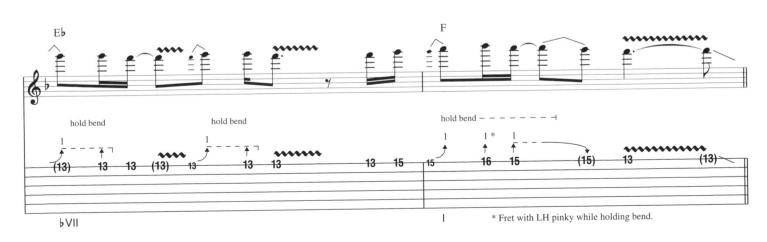

* Fret with LH pinky while holding bend.

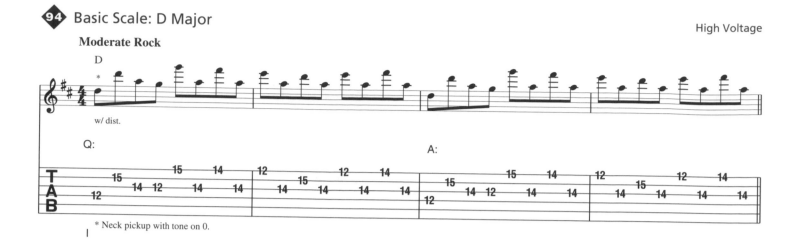

◆94 Basic Scale: D Major

Moderate Rock

* Neck pickup with tone on 0.

◆95 Basic Scale: E Phrygian Dominant

Moderate Rock

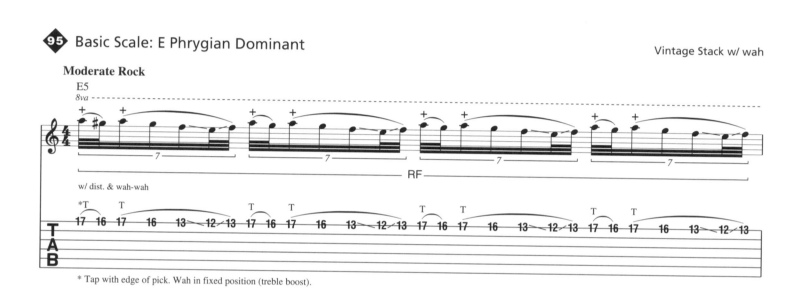

w/ dist. & wah-wah

* Tap with edge of pick. Wah in fixed position (treble boost).

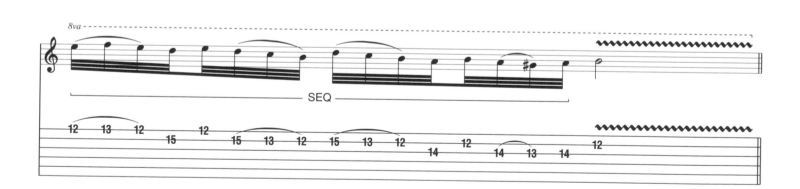

The Nineties

The nineties were a tumultuous period for rock guitar. Eric Johnson, a genuine rock guitar virtuoso, raised existing musical standards overnight with his *Ah Via Musicom* recording. The Seattle *grunge* movement of the early nineties reintroduced a punk-oriented simplicity to rock guitar that was missing in the guitar hero era of eighties. Kurt Cobain with Nirvana and a host of bands like Pearl Jam, Stone Temple Pilots, Soundgarden, and Alice In Chains ultimately gave rise to the *alternative rock* movement of the mid to late nineties. Subsequent alternative rock guitarists include Mark Tremonti (Creed), Tom Morello (Rage Against The Machine), and Wes Borland (Limp Bizkit). The nineties also saw a renewed interest in classic rock guitarists like Eric Clapton, Jeff Beck, and Carlos Santana.

These licks were played on my rock warhorses: a Fender Jeff Beck Strat and a Gibson Les Paul sunburst Standard. The amp settings ranged from vintage stack sounds to processed tones like Cliffs (EQ, echo, and reverb) and modern stacks.

96 Basic Tonality: G Major

Cliffs

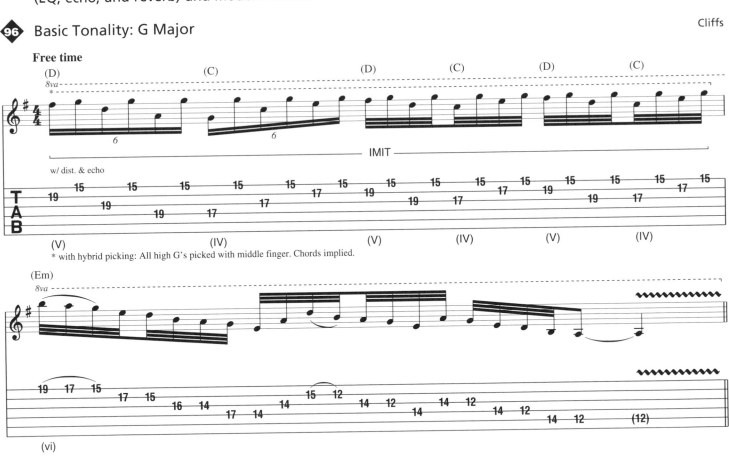

* with hybrid picking: All high G's picked with middle finger. Chords implied.

97 Basic Scale: G Major

Cliffs

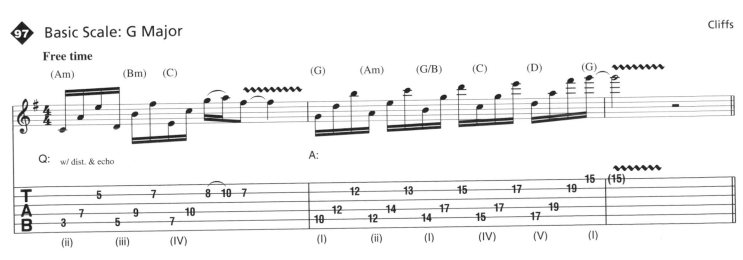

43

98 Basic Scale: F♯ Minor

Dual Richter w/ Triangle Chorus & Reverb

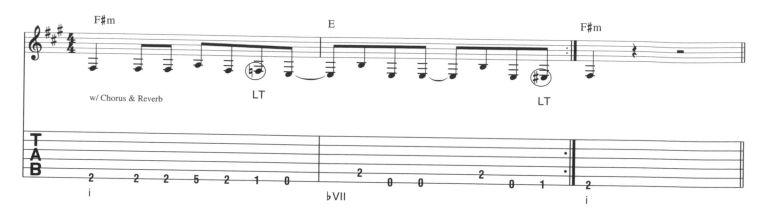

99 Basic Scale: E Minor Pentatonic

Vintage Stack & Wah Pedal

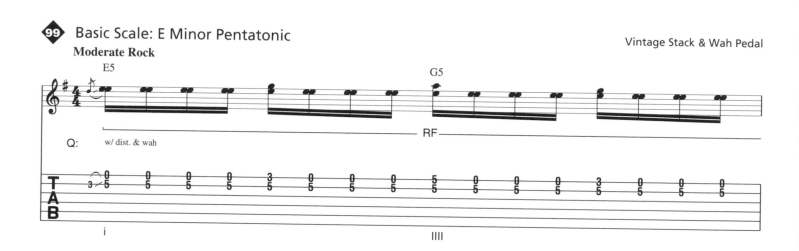

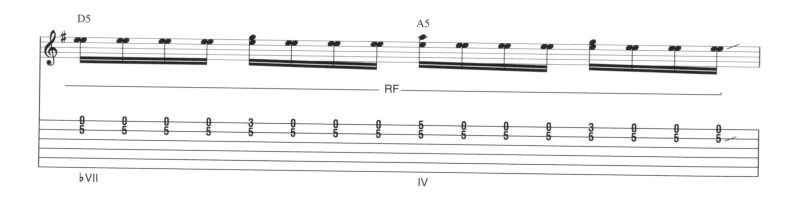

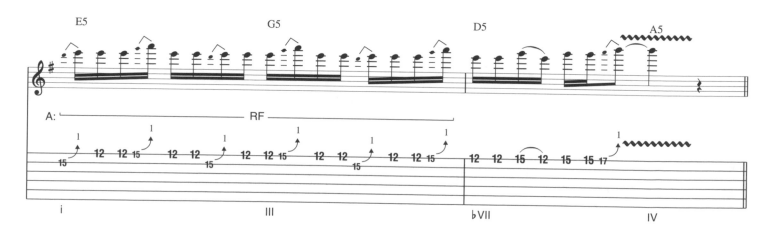

44

[Lick 100]
Basic Tonality: D Major

Modern Stack

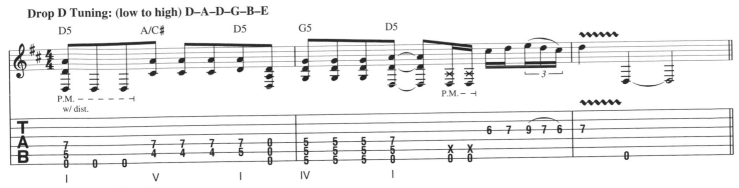

Drop D Tuning: (low to high) D–A–D–G–B–E

* Lick 100 begins at 0:46 of Track 99.

[Lick 101]
Basic Scale: A Harmonic Minor/ Natural Minor

Big Wet Lead

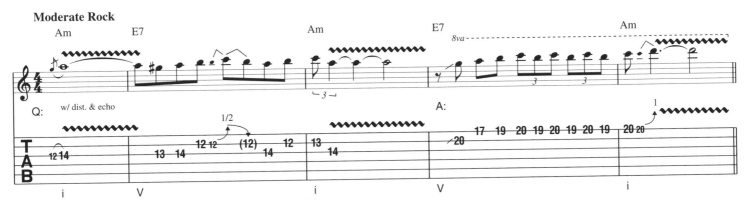

* Lick 100 begins at 1:16 of Track 99.

Suggested Recordings

Studying music is a lifelong commitment. If you wish to explore the rock genre more thoroughly, here are some definitive guitar recordings filled with must-know licks offered for your continuing study and appreciation.

Chuck Berry:
: *The Great Twenty-Eight* (Chess).
  The Chess Box (Chess).

Scotty Moore:
: *The Sun Sessions—Elvis Presley* (RCA).
  Elvis: The King of Rock 'n' Roll: Complete '50s Masters (RCA).

Carl Perkins:
: *Original Sun Greatest Hits* (Rhino).

Cliff Gallup:
: *Gene Vincent Box Set* (EMI).

James Burton:
: *Ricky Nelson: Legendary Masters* (EMI).

Bo Diddley:
: *The Chess Box* (Charly).

Buddy Holly:
: *The Buddy Holly Collection* (MCA).

Brian Setzer:
: *Best of the Stray Cats: Rock This Town* (EMI).

Various:
: *Rock This Town: Rockabilly Hits, Vol.1 and Vol.2* (Rhino).

Various:
: *Rock Instrumentals* (Rhino).

The Beatles:
: *With the Beatles* (Capitol).
  Rubber Soul (Capitol).
  Revolver (Capitol).
  Sgt. Pepper's Lonely Hearts Club Band (Capitol).
  The Beatles (The White Album) (Capitol).
  Abbey Road (Capitol).

The Rolling Stones:
: *Sticky Fingers* (Virgin).
  Exile on Main Street (Virgin).
  Tattoo You (Virgin).

Eric Clapton:
: *Cream: Disraeli Gears* (Polydor).
  Cream: Wheels of Fire (Polydor).

Jeff Beck:
: *Truth* (Epic).
  Beckology (Epic).

Jimi Hendrix:
: *Are You Experienced* (Reprise).
  Axis: Bold As Love (Reprise).
  Electric Ladyland (Reprise).
  Band of Gypsys (Capitol).
  Radio One (Rykodisc).

Jimmy Page:
: *Led Zeppelin Boxed Set* (Atlantic).
  Led Zeppelin Box Set 2 (Atlantic).

Carlos Santana:
: *Santana* (Columbia).
  Abraxas (Columbia).
  Dance of the Rainbow Serpent (Columbia).

Ritchie Blackmore:	*Deep Purple: Machine Head* (Warner Bros.)
Tony Iommi:	*Black Sabbath: We Sold Our Souls For Rock And Roll* (Warner Bros).
David Gilmour:	*Pink Floyd: Dark Side Of The Moon* (Capitol). *Pink Floyd: The Wall* (Columbia).
Michael Schenker:	*MSG* (Chrysalis).
Uli Roth:	*Scorpions: Tokyo Tapes* (RCA).
Allan Holdsworth:	*I.O.U.* (Enigma).
Al DiMeola:	*Return To Forever* (Elektra)
Brian May:	*Queen: Greatest Hits* (Hollywood).
Joe Walsh:	*The Eagles: Hotel California* (Asylum).
Gary Moore:	*Victims Of The Future* (Relativity).
Billy Gibbons:	*The Best of ZZ Top* (Warner Bros.).
Angus Young:	*AC/DC: Back in Black* (Atco).
Larry Carlton:	*Steely Dan: The Royal Scam* (MCA). *Larry Carlton* (MCA).
Eddie Van Halen:	*Van Halen* (Warner Bros.). *Van Halen II* (Warner Bros.). *Women and Children First* (Warner Bros.). *Fair Warning* (Warner Bros.). *1984* (Warner Bros.).
Randy Rhoads:	*Ozzy Osbourne: Blizzard of Ozz* (Jet). *Ozzy Osbourne: Diary of a Madman* (Jet). *Ozzy Osbourne/Randy Rhoads: Tribute* (Epic).
Yngwie Malmsteen:	*Alcatrazz: No Parole from Rock 'n' Roll* (Rocshire). *Rising Force* (Polydor).
Steve Morse:	*High Tension Wires* (MCA). *Southern Steel* (MCA).
Steve Vai:	*Flex-able* (Akashic). *Passion and Warfare* (Relativity).
Joe Satriani:	*Surfing with the Alien* (Relativity).
Steve Lukather:	*Toto: IV* (Columbia).
Slash:	*Guns N' Roses: Appetite for Destruction* (Geffen).
Kirk Hammett:	*Metallica: Metallica* (Elektra).
Eric Johnson:	*Ah Via Musicom* (Reprise).
Kurt Cobain:	*Nevermind* (DGC).
Pearl Jam:	*Ten* (Epic).
Mark Tremonti:	*Creed: My Own Prison* (Wind Up) *Creed: Human Clay* (Wind Up)
Tom Morello:	*Rage Against The Machine: Evil Empire* (Epic).

About the Author

Wolf Marshall is the pre-eminent guitar educator-performer of our time. The founder and original editor-in-chief of *GuitarOne* magazine, he is a highly respected and prolific author and columnist who has been an influential force in music education since the early 1980s. Wolf has worked closely with Hal Leonard Corporation for the last decade and authored such acclaimed multimedia books as *The Guitar Style of Stevie Ray Vaughan, Best of The Doors, Blues Guitar Classics, The Beatles Favorites, The Beatles Hits, The Rolling Stones, The Best of Carlos Santana, Guitar Instrumental Hits, Steve Vai: Alien Love Secrets, Eric Clapton Unplugged, Eric Johnson, The Guitars of Elvis, Aerosmith 1973-1979* and *Aerosmith 1979-1998, The Guitar Style of Mark Knopfler, The Best of Queen, The Best of Cream, Wes Montgomery, The Best of Jazz*, and many more. His eight-volume series *The Wolf Marshall Guitar Method* and *Power Studies* established new standards for modern guitar pedagogy in the early 1990s, as did his popular *Guitar Jammin'* authentic song books.

In *101 Must-Know Rock Licks*—and its predecessors, *101 Must-Know Jazz Licks* and *101 Must-Know Blues Licks*—Wolf directs his encyclopedic knowledge of modern guitar music at a unique stylistic series designed to improve and expand the vocabulary of all guitarists. The list of his credits is immense and can be found at his web site: *www.wolfmarshall.com.*